MORNING STAR RISING

MORNING STAR RISING
a book of poetry

by Sanseria Murray

MORNING STAR RISING
a b o o k o f p o e t r y
by Sanseria Murray

www.SonStarProductions.com

PUBLISHED BY

That'll Write Books

publisher@SonStarProductions.com

Library of Congress Control Number: 2021914888
ISBN 978-0-5789298-5-9

Book design by Kimball Productions
Story editing by Jen Wentlandt
Cover photos by Brandon Concepcion
Headshots of the author by Paul Ballain

Manufactured in the United States of America
First Edition

CONTENTS

DEDICATION

For those who struggle with loneliness, wrestle with God, touch the face of beauty, yearn for something more and discover it within.

For those still chasing dreams and finding purpose, May you uncover your light and turn it ALL the way up.

For Black people, my ancestors whose hands I hold, I honor your courage, strength, and resilience, May we know our beauty and magic.

For women who have been silenced, May you discover your voice and the courage to speak.

For queer people who feel trapped in hopeless despair, May you find comfort in community.

Morning Star Rising

For my fellow sinners and believers,
May you know the real presence of God and be
swept away in Their glory and Great Love.

For my students
May you discover the power of your own voice.

For the poor,
May you know the many riches of love.
For those struggling artists,
May you becoming thriving, abundant artists.

For those of us who face fear in the dark and live to
see the dawn.

For those of us still learning and growing and still
have questions.

I am for you.

This is for you.

ACKNOWLEDGMENTS

It is with a full heart that thanks goes to my Aunt Joyce who was proud of me *before* the book was published. Thank you for showing me how to catch a dream.

Huge thanks to Gabby, my number one cheerleader. I'm so grateful to have shared this process with you.

I appreciate you, Andrea "Vocab" Sanderson. Your light shines SO bright. I am honored by your brilliance.

Deep gratitude goes to Brandon Concepcion. Thank you for lending your visual artistry and creative energy to this project.

Big thanks to Jen Wentlandt, my awesome editor and faithful friend for making sure (or is it ensuring?) that all my i's were dotted and the t's were crossed.

The incredible team at Kimball Productions, my heart is overwhelmed with gratitude for y'all. Thank you for the gift of seeing myself in such a beautiful and powerful way. Tom and Ben - it was such an uplifting experience to be able to work with your creative team! My cup is truly running over.

PREFACE

Since I can remember, I've been captivated by words. Words are my passion. I'm fascinated by language. I am a word nerd. The lure of language, alliteration, metaphor, rhyme and rhythm; I was enthralled! So began the affair with poetry and it gave way to a gripping love story.

Our words have power. How they hurt. How they heal. How the power of words wielded thoughtfully, can bring universes into being.

I am also a hopeful romantic. I'm always discovering poetry in everything: good food, soft rain, a long embrace, an engaging conversation.

Although I began writing poetry in middle school, the idea for this book has been stewing for more than fifteen years. While it took several years for the book to become the story it wanted to tell, it wasn't until 2019 that I finally put pen to paper for Morning Star Rising.

Shortly thereafter, the whole world turned upside down. The simmering of racial injustice came to a full, rolling boil.

There was so much trauma around the presidential election and the insurrection on the capitol that followed. Our world seemed to be spiraling towards an abyss vacant of love. It felt like we lost our way: holding ethnic groups in contempt, writing each other off as if we didn't, in fact, belong to each other.

Anxiety knows no age limts. Sorrow transcends race. We are all more alike than we are different. There is something magnificent in unique oneness that is different than in dull sameness.

This book is my attempt to add an example of living in radical love. I believe our lives follow a cycle: suffering, love, healing... suffering, love, healing...

When school finally started again, I taught my students an affirmation which we recited daily. I wanted my students to have a deep understanding, a heart knowledge that we need one another to survive and to thrive. It was my desire to convey to them the beauty in diversity.

It is my hope that in this book you will find love in these words. You will find hope in your sorrow, joy in your lament, and gratitude in your grief.

Read this affirmation with me...

I am light.

I am loved.

We are one.

I belong to you.

You belong to me.

We are one.

PROLOGUE

Cosmos

Dance away with me
Into the supernova
Love all consuming

Black. Woman. Queer. Christian. Teacher. Poor. Artist.

Though these labels may describe me, I long to bust out of the restricting box they place me in. I want to explode far and wide in a vast expanse of love. My desire is to live in a space that is beyond labels that do not reveal the whole of who I am.

Labels reduce our stardust...

So I am not big on labels.

My name is Sanseria. "It means morning star." My mother would often remind me that my name was beautiful. Different yes, but not hard. "Son-see-ah-ray". My name is constantly mispronounced. I often find myself explaining the origin, spelling it phonetically for people and saying it very slowly.

S a n s e r i a.

Glory

-isms break my heart
Your label cannot define
I am glorious

So many labels have negative connotations. Yet we consistently label people to compartmentalize them into categories that make them (seemingly) better understood. Isn't there more humanity to us than labels?

It is my hope that by reading this work, you will have a better understanding of who we can be without the confines of labels. After all, we have all loved and lost. We have all suffered and healed (or at least are coping). We're all afraid of something. The dark. Death. Losing a lover. A job. We are all embarrassed about something. The stretch marks. The fact that you were a bully in sixth grade.

We all hope for something.

And we all love something.

I Love You

When I say I love you
I am saying no to fear
Fear that grasps the
reality of
Us
And chokes it into the lie
That I am not worthy of love
Not worthy of loving or being loved

I love you
Saying these words are
Permission granted to be
Wild
Free
Unbridled passion
Into fierce action and
Empathetic compassion

I love you
The sound of the words falling
Past my lips is
The cool quench to my parched soul

I love you

I love you

I love me enough to acknowledge
The light in you
I love you
I recognize your hurt and pain
I recognize your joy and fear

I love you
I will not
Abandon myself to death
By failing to say
I love you

I love you
And I mean it

ACT I
GREAT SUFFERING

Shame

Suddenly the shame
Knocking at my heart once more
An unwelcomed guest

Many of our journeys include tragic hardships. Mine is not unlike yours, in that I have had to endure suffering. Early in my sorrow, I searched for someone or something bigger than me. Bigger than the abuse of my father. Bigger than the insults and ridicule of my fourth grade teacher. Bigger than the scary shadows at night. Bigger than my mother's voice. My eyes desperately scanned the horizon looking for my rescuer. I longed for someone to ride in, reach down, and rescue me from this hellish rut. My feet were cement bricks in quicksand and fighting was futile. I had to hold onto hope or surely I would have died in hopeless despair.

Captive

How can I be
      free

If I am the very
          captive
               of
                   me

Truth

How do you tell the
            truth
When the truth is not
            beautiful

When it is ugly and
            hateful
Despicable rotting
            eating stink
A haunting nightmare
            desperate to awake
            and escape

Perhaps to deny
is to survive

And to sleep is to
rest with one eye
            open

If I can't accept
            or admit
then how can
            I cope
                with
                    a ghost?

Silence

How can I be so loud
and no one hear

Silence so loud

Funny thing silence

Silence holds you
prisoner

Silence pierces your
heart and bleeds
you quietly

Silence chokes the
life out of you

Silence makes
denial so loud

Silence lingers
and creeps
and snuffs out
        truth

Silence lies and
tells you the unthinkable
is buried

Silence unearths it
rehearses it
Silence re-lives it
breathes life into it

Silence tells you
over and over
        again.

Silence murders truth

Who Will

Who will hold me
      now?
Who will kiss my
      tears?
Now that I am
      face to face
      with fear?

Who will comfort my
      sick?
Who can see through
      this haze so
      thick?

Who will believe my
      abuse?
Who will understand
      my
         truth?

Where do I go from
      here?
What happens now?
How do I heal?
My soul cries
      out
to be whole

How long will you
        only see
My dancing eyes
And smile so
        wide

What about the hole
        inside
And the pain I
        hide
The tragedy I
        disguise
The wicked lies
Why can't I just
        say good-bye
to the hurt
to find my worth

No one sees – me

And so it goes

I laugh out
        loud

And cry
        alone.

If you were to hold a five pound weight out in front of your chest, it probably wouldn't feel so heavy. At first.

After holding it out with a straight arm in front of you, for say, five minutes, it would seem heavier.

In that short five minutes, your muscles would begin to tense. Your shoulders would tighten. Your arm may start to fall. Your fingers would hold fast to the weight, tightening their grip, so as not to drop it.

The rest of your body's energy is focused on the weight in front of you. Perhaps your breath quickens. You may shift your own body weight from right to left.

Five minutes, turns to ten minutes, and the weight seems unbearable. The weight has not changed. It is still just five pounds.

In this way, weight is not unlike wait. Time can be eagerly anticipated.

The arrival of a long-awaited lover. The birth of a child you've expected for months.

Or waiting can be tortuous.

Waiting on news from a job interview or a call from the doctor.

A few years ago, I had a breast biopsy. After quite a few mammograms, and ultrasounds the doctor decided a biopsy of the lump would be best.

Waiting for the pathology report seemed like an eternity. Minutes became hours that stretched into days which grew heavier with each moment. Each inhale came with a new worry that held the exhale captive. My already white-knuckled grip on what this long awaited call may mean began to tighten. All of my energy was holding fast to the ringing of the phone. Bated breath. Rapid heartbeat.

My arm would surely give out at any moment.

The Wait

I know it will be great
After this long, painful wait

When the hurting subsides
And I can see again
I'll be able to breathe,
And dream and really live

I would risk it all
All just one more time
If I knew all that God
Had in store
It is so worth
waiting for

Cuz it's gonna be so great
After this long, winter wait
When the sun comes out
To warm my face and
melt away my doubt

This icy loneliness seems
too much to take
the burden of failure
is heavy with weight

Frozen in cold silence
only to hear the echo
of my heartache

Don't know if I'll ever
see past these bare trees
and fallen leaves
what waits for me

What waits for me?

What waits for me
He waits for me

Cuz it's been so long
and I didn't think
I was this strong
What a great wait
what a great weight
has been lifted from me
and carried away on His love
a purpose so big
I'd've never
thought of

What a great wait
How long do you wait?
What to do while I wait...

In the stillness I find movement
In the stillness I find peace
In the stillness I find you
waiting

for

me

Sanseria Murray

ACT II
GREAT LOVE

Mirror

Radiance you shine
Your love is the truth I see
In my reflection

The Great Spirit of Love and Kindness has been revealed to me in many faces. My life is full up with Framily. Friends who have become family = Framily. We often celebrate with Friendsgiving each year in November. We come together around birthdays and babies. We live life together in a way that is real, authentic and messy. This kind of love has changed the trajectory of my life.

Like love, a sunrise warms, purifies, and gives life. I am in part, the sum of those who have impacted me deeply and have brightened my life with their love. My brother, the diamond. My sister, the sparkle. And I, the sun. Sanseria, the morning star rising. More. I am a galaxy of love.

This love has spurred me on to be the teacher that has had a great impact on my students. This love has compelled me to be the best version of myself. To love and be loved; to know and be known, is the desire of our hearts. This love has in fact, saved my life time and again.

My sister. We met at a Christian youth camp in 1987. Both had struggling single moms. We were latch-key kids and she had been raised as an only child. We have been inseparable from the moment we met. I helped her raise her kids after her first marriage ended in divorce. She helped me rebuild my life after chronic illness threatened to take me out.

There is no better friend than a sister, and no better sister than her.

The seeds of what romantic love could be, came in the way of a gentle young man, my boyfriend in high school. He was not violent or demanding like my previous boyfriends. He would surprise me with white roses. We would sing along to our songs whenever Chicago would play on the radio.

And then there was Her. The One I thought I'd spend my life with after a short lived experience in love. My feelings for her would only further fuel my passion for advocacy.

Babe. I carry with me 30 years of love and friendship with him. The reminder; a simple silver bracelet he purchased in Mexico and placed on my wrist in 1995. He has loved me through tragedy and triumph. Loss of jobs, loss of parents, loss of love. We have gained so much through our life-long friendship - laughing as we reminisce of the many fond memories to draw from.

My cousin. My favorite person. My heart is eternally grateful for the man who has loved me and always sees the best in me; especially when I have trouble seeing it in myself. He is encouraging, empowering and inspiring. One of the most powerful, creative storytellers I know, he is a true gift in my life. He has shown me what it means to love and embrace myself, compelling me to growth.

Sink

Loving you feels like home
When I turn toward the loving
Go deep to the knowing
There is nothing to do but love you

On the surface there is a
chaos of questions
How could this be?
On the surface there is "what if" bargaining
What if I'm really not his type?
On the surface the cacophony of confusion
sweeps over me
Again and again
And again
and again
Wave after wave
Crashing me in the face
I can't breathe
Go deep
A voice says from within
Another wave
Crashing

Crushing
Forcing me down
Perhaps the ocean knows
I need to get deep

Down deep
I can breathe
Calm washes over me
As floating and sinking both occur

I love you
I will love you everyday for the rest of my life
because loving you is going deep

Loving you requires my action of surrender
to the deep
Loving you demands that I swim in the deep
knowing
Knowing
Trusting
Allowing
Fearless

In this deep stillness

There is a quiet resilience
Like a RE-silencing
Like being still
And knowing

There below the surface
There in the deep still part of me
Is you

And we dance
Cheek to cheek
Slowly
Softly
Deliberately

We cry
Snot faced and hot breathed
We cry
Loudly
Silently

We laugh
With not nary a lick of sense
Whole mouth

Whole body
We laugh

We inhale
Each other's eyes
Drinking in the soul of the other and recog-
nizing our own
Your eyes peer into mine
Vulnerable
Exposed
A gentle gaze
I see you

Loving me
Loving you
Loving me

It goes on like this
Drinking each other in
Realizing we are the
Ocean

The Framily - Through my Brother-Husbands - I've been blessed beyond measure to know them as a father, husband, brother, and friend. Each of them inspire me, challenge me and comfort me. I can count on them for spiritual advice, financial counsel, a hearty laugh (always with the shenanigans!), business organization, (and sometimes jobs!); they always have my back.

Whether it's to fix my car, my resume, or even my heart. They may not know it, but I have experienced a great deal of healing through our relationships. They have re-parented me. God has brought me a great deal of healing by watching them parent their own children.

I've seen what it is to be a father of playfulness, of discipline, with secure attachment for your children. In them, I see sacrifice, humility and a fierce love and protection for their families, which includes me.

It has been said that you can know yourself based on the joy in someone else's eyes as they look at you. I see the delight in my Sister-Friend's eyes when they answer the door and discover it's me on the other side. These Sister-Friends remind me what it is like me to act. They are constantly pointing me back to love, joy and grace.

These women are my tribe. My village who rallies around me to support, lift up and even protect. They have shared their children with me.

These families are home to me. I love and respect my Brother-Husbands. I have a deep gratitude for my Sister-Friends. I love the way they look out for me, pray for me, support me through lightness and dark;

thick and thin. And for showing me who GOD is by their friendship and kinship.

The sheer joy reflected in all my children's smiles upon greeting their Aunt Cece is truly priceless! Easily one of the greatest treasures of my life has been to love and be loved as Aunt Cece.

As a teacher, my students have taught me what it is to rise and shine through their own brilliance. They are my forever students.

Not ever having my own children these students are my legacy. I have learned from them as much as they have learned from me.

Sanseria Murray

You Child

You child
with your wild curiosity,
you provoke me to questioning

You child
with your big imagination,
you lead me to inspiration

You child
with your insightful thoughts,
you teach me wisdom

You child
with your endless energy,
you take me on adventures

You child
with your fearless bravery,
you give me boldness

You child
with your giggly laughs,
you increase my joy

You child
with your surprising answers,
you show me knowledge

You child
    fascinate me
    encourage me
    challenge me

And with your gentle
    kindness
You child
captivate me
    with
        love.

Sanseria Murray

ACT III
GREAT HEALING

River

Her river calls me
Drowning my sorrow within
Collection of tears

In what turned out to be "The Beginning" of my healing process close friends, a married couple, began inviting me over to their home for the weekends. I was living in Southern California. I must have been in my mid-twenties. The home included: dad and mama, and their two children: a daughter (4-years-old at the time) and a son (just a year old); and Poppy and Grammy, my friend's parents who lived downstairs.

While I don't remember when the weekend visits started, the one thing I do know for sure, those weekends began a deep healing for me.

Weekends typically started on Friday, with the at least hour-long commute from West LA to Highland Park. In the car, the dad and I would talk about theology, argue over who was the better team: Spurs versus Lakers (Spurs, of course). We talked about politics and church stuff. He challenged me in such a gentle way about what I believed and why.

Saturdays consisted of loads of laundry, Target runs, games with the kids, reading to them, dishes and dinner. Around their kitchen table, I learned to make enchiladas, play Scribbage with Grammy, soak up the wisdom of Poppy, and observed what a healthy family looked like.

I remember feeling grafted into their family tree. It's where I became Aunt Cece. It's where the dawn had broken into the dark night of my soul. The broken bits got sorted out and like a puzzle, the straight-edge pieces that make the frame, got put together.

These people weren't perfect. They were real, honest and invited me to live life with them. I saw the rawness of their family and it was beautiful.

A few years later, I found myself in what I now refer to as "The Wilderness." After a devastating break up, I began a 15 year journey through a desert of self-discovery. I took the time to explore who I am, what and why I believe what I do and the reason behind my actions. I realized that I was becoming who I had always been.

It was a real wrestling time. An uncertain time. A wandering around in the struggle of loneliness. I was angry with God. I spent so much time groping in the darkness until I decided to turn the light in me all the way up. I had to go through a deconstruction of who God was/is.

Then, in Their infinite wisdom, They wooed me back to reconstruction. I was determined to have beauty for ashes.

Psalm 30, verse 11, says, "You have changed my sadness into a joyful dance; you have taken away my sorrow and surrounded me with joy."

As the book of Romans reminds me, I can boast in the hope I have found in God. I can also boast in my suffering because I know that suffering produces perseverance; perseverance produces character and character produces hope. This hope does not disappoint!

Sanseria Murray

The Hope

My grief has swallowed me up
I can only lament over
loved ones lost
dreams dried up
families torn apart
love sought
and not
returned
This is the burden of heart

Suddenly I feel a spark
something deep down
in my soul so dark
a glimmer, a hope

The Spirit is calling me
reminding me
reshaping me

renewing me
restoring me

I was so completely devastated
drowning in my own sorrow
And now there is hope

Hope like tomorrow

Hope like
Your Spirit leads me on

Hope like
peace when all else is
chaos and calamity

Hope like
When I pass through the waters
they will not overtake me

Hope like
When I walk through the fire
I shall not be burned

Hope like
No weapon formed against me shall prosper

Hope like
I can slay giants
and rest with lions

Hope like
I can stand firm
for you are with me

Here I was
desperate and alone
And now there is hope
Hope in the One
The One who clothes
The One who covers
The One who discovers
the hurt
and heals

The One who was broken
so I could be
made whole
The One who defied darkness
and saved my soul

My ache was so great
with no end
in sight
not a friend
or light
only surrounded by pain
what was I to gain
after losing so much
I cried out for a touch
From the One who sets the captive free
allows me to live so abundantly
and loves me so completely

And now there is something
where there was nothing.

Hope. Hope.

Hope.

The world-wide pandemic of Covid-19 led to a lockdown quarantine of more than eighteen weeks. Surprisingly, I cherished the time I had in the quarantine. It was an invitation to the Great Pause.

I have learned to embrace who I am. Flaws and all. During the quarantine of the Great Pause, I was again reminded that I was becoming who I already was. To be clear, this work is never done. During the quarantine, I described the weeks alone in my apartment as a cocooning of sorts. A delicious honeymoon with me, myself and I.

In my solitude, I read books, watched documentaries, and listened to podcasts. This silence was different. It was a glorious time of creative expression. Journaled prayers became poetry which begat watercolor paintings, and then more poetry. I listened to great books. *More Myself* by Alicia Keys. *Untamed* by Glennon Doyle.

I have Glennon to thank for inspiring the following piece.

The Lion Declaration

I have to say it out loud. I need to say it to me. I need to say it aloud so that I hear it. I need to say it to you so you can remind me when I forget.

I am a lion. I'm a damn lion!

In this moment and every moment after this, I never want to forget who I am. I am bold. I am fierce. I am untamed. I am glory.

I do not want to settle. I don't, and I can't, and I won't settle for anything less than my best life. I will feel all the feelings. I will be present to the moments as scary as they may be and as exhausted as I may be; I will show up to life.

I will no longer yearn for something beautiful I only caught a glimpse of in my dreamer's imagination. I will instead make decisions and take action knowing that my imagination is not the place to go to escape reality, but that my holy imagination is the place I go to discover my truest reality.

I will stop choosing suffering. I will not worship my pain. I will not wear my suffering like a name badge I have to continue to explain how to pronounce. I will not participate in comparative suffering, now knowing that my suffering is the one that matters. What is happening to me and what it left me with is mine alone to process.

I will stop explaining. I will stop justifying. I will stop defending. I will lean into lament. And I will take as long as it takes. I will seek to understand and be understood.

I will stop selling myself short. I will not shrink in the silhouette of my full stature. I will breathe to fill my lungs and not worry about being too big or taking up too much space. No more playing small.

I will love in a full out sprint. I will love with everything I've got. I will not be shy about who or why or how I love. I will love with a no-holds-barred, extravagant, messy kind of love. And that includes loving myself that way.

I will allow joy. I will laugh with my whole self. I will lean into joy without probating it.

And when I'm called on to be brave and I feel I can't muster the strength, I will take a deep breath and remember:

I am a LION!

Sanseria Murray

EPILOGUE

Astronaut

Morning Star Rising
Our words, our stars, who we are
Take us to the moon

We all have a story. A story of victory, triumph, and overcoming. My story isn't over yet. We have all loved and lost. We have all suffered and healed. We have all survived. We are all still growing. It's okay to grow slow.

My healing story continues. Now I strive to stand in the full stature of who God is calling me to be. Surely there will be more suffering to endure. Perhaps there will be more great love. If, as we all engage in our internal work, maybe we can see more grace and kindness and the humanity in each other? We just might be able to see past the labels we assign to each other. We may be a witness to the miraculous.

Miracles happen everyday through extraordinary love. Breathe with me. Put your hand on your heart and whisper these words to yourself, "I am a miracle".

Miracle

I am a miracle
It is a mystery how you found me

Struggling alone
In the darkness of abuse
Engulfed in the pain of my past
Drowning in sorrow
Tormented, at war within

I could barely breathe
Life was slipping away

Then you
All of you

Not appearing as if you haven't always
been there
Not moving as if you weren't already
in motion

Just you

You with your light
Your brilliance
Your radiance
You shone on me

You
Your love
Unconditional, kind, boundless, unfailing
Your love washed over me

You
Your grace
Perfect, amazing, surrounding, favor
You forgave me

You
Your mercy
Good, compassionate, free
You pardoned me

You
Your faithfulness
Always knowing, ever present, providing

You
All of you
And I
became a miracle

Reaching out toward you
and finding you inside
Where you abide

You
You rescue
You
You save
You
You gave
me
All of you

And now
Color is coming back to my face
And breath is returning to my lungs
Blood is pumping through my veins
Life is coming, Life is here
Right here, Right now

I am present to your presence
the marvelous work of your hand
the design of me
the shape of me
the beauty of me

the miracle of me

Beloved,

Many blessings to you, reader. May you find the strength, joy, and courage to shed your labels and write your own story. I'll be here in these pages, sending you love and light.

Sanseria

Sanseria Murray